Office 201

The Premiere User Guide
for Work, Home & Play.

Cheat Sheets Edition:
Hacks, Tips, Shortcuts & Tricks.

Standard Ordinary Human

Solutions & Training, 20-year Microsoft Veteran

Office 2016 for Beginners

Release: 1.0.1.3c

Table of Contents

About Ordinary Human

Ordinary Human is a 20-year veteran of Microsoft who previously worked with various Microsoft teams to write documentation for Windows, Windows Server and other Microsoft products. If you have ever used any Microsoft product or operating system or had Microsoft training, you've probably seen Ordinary Human's work in action.

Ordinary Human pledges to update this manual from time to time to make corrections and changes as Office 2016 changes, and to add content. How much time Ordinary Human can dedicate to the book depends on its readership and participation from readers like you.

Introduction

When it comes to technology and computers, ordinary humans often need a little help getting through the day. Sometimes ordinary humans wish training manuals had just the steps needed to get the job done and that's exactly what you'll find in this handy quick reference guide filled with step-by-step instructions and shortcuts for how to use Microsoft Office 2016.

Not only does this book provide a streamlined and concise learning experience, it is also an easy to use reference guide for any type of user that will help you get the job done quickly. Using this guide, you'll be able to:

- Teach yourself the essentials and latest features
- Learn how the new Office works
- Work more efficiently with Office 2016
- Find just the tasks you need

Flying Start

Throughout this guide, where we use CLICK, RIGHT-CLICK and DOUBLE-CLICK, you can use the touch equivalents of TAP, PRESS AND HOLD and DOUBLE TAP. HOVER means to position the mouse over the designated item without CLICKING.

When working in Tablet mode, CLICK START should be replaced with CLICK ![icon] on the START screen.

![windows logo] This is the Windows Logo Key on your keyboard. Press this key in combination with other keys to access keyboard shortcuts. Press this key by itself to display or hide Start.

When starting and using Word, Excel or PowerPoint without a document, the start screen provides options for creating a new document or opening an existing document. If you have a file open already, CLICK FILE, NEW or CLICK FILE, OPEN for similar options.

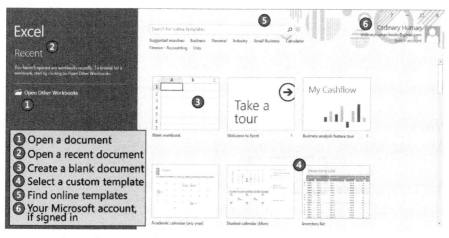

① Open a document
② Open a recent document
③ Create a blank document
④ Select a custom template
⑤ Find online templates
⑥ Your Microsoft account, if signed in

You don't have to use a Microsoft account with Office 2016. However, having one allows you to save and share your documents online for access by other people, or on other devices. A Microsoft account also allows you to install and use Office add-ins, such as a dictionary or consistency checker.

To sign in:

1. Choose FILE, ACCOUNT.

2. CLICK **Sign In** , then follow the instructions for signing in or creating an account.

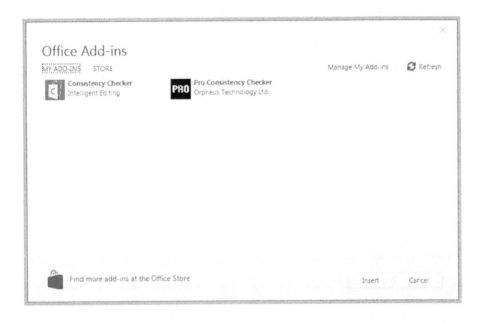

When you are signed in, you can get add-ins from the Microsoft store. To install add-ins:

1. CLICK INSERT, **Store**.
2. Search for add-ins and CLICK an add-in to view its details page.
3. CLICK TRUST IT.

To use add-ins:

1. CLICK INSERT, **My Add-ins**.
2. The Office Add-Ins dialog box shows available add-ins.

3. CLICK the add-in to use, then CLICK **Insert**.

Working with the Ribbon

The Ribbon displays along the top of the window in Word, Excel and PowerPoint. Use the tabs to display groups of related commands. Keep in mind some tabs, such as Table Tools and Picture Tools, only appear when you select a table or picture.

CLICK the Show Dialog button in a group to display additional options. For example, CLICK the Show Dialog button in the Font group to display additional font options.

Changing How the Ribbon Displays

While it's handy to have the ribbon open at all times, the ribbon takes up a lot of space and you may want to control its display. You can work with the ribbon in several ways.

- To collapse the ribbon, CLICK on the right side of the ribbon.
- To temporarily show a collapsed ribbon, CLICK a tab on the ribbon. You can then select a command.
- Alternatively, show or hide the collapsed ribbon by pressing CTRL + F1.

To keep the ribbon open while you work, pin it:

1. CLICK a tab on the title bar.

2. CLICK .

Hiding the Ribbon Completely

To completely hide the ribbon:

1. CLICK on the right side of the title bar.
2. CLICK Auto-Hide Ribbon.

CLICK in the title bar to display a hidden ribbon or press and hold ALT.

To stop hiding the ribbon:

1. CLICK on the right side of the title bar.
2. CLICK Show Tabs or Show Tabs And Commands.

Using the Quick Access Toolbar

The Quick Access toolbar is displayed on the left side of the ribbon.

The default options are:

- **Save**   Saves the open document
- **Undo**   Undoes the last action
- **Repeat / Redo**   Repeats or redoes the last action
- **Customize**   Displays options for adding or removing buttons

Any command on any tab or toolbar can be added to quick access. To add a command, RIGHT-CLICK the command on a tab or other ribbon location, then select Add To Quick Access Toolbar.

To remove a command, RIGHT-CLICK the command on the quick access toolbar, then select Remove From Quick Access Toolbar.

Optimizing for Touch UI

You can optimize the ribbon for either mouse and keyboard or touch mode. To add the Touch/Mouse Mode button to Quick Access:

1. CLICK ▼ on the Quick Access toolbar.
2. CLICK Touch/Mouse Mode.

With the Touch/Mouse button added to Quick Access, CLICK

, then CLICK Touch.

With touch UI mode, commands are larger and have more space between them. Some commands change from using button/drop-down combinations to using only drop-downs.

To use Mouse Mode instead, CLICK , then CLICK Mouse.

Working with Document Windows

Each document you open in an Office application is opened in a separate window.

Opening a New Document Window

Opening a new window opens a blank document in the Office application.

- CLICK View, then CLICK New Window.

Switching Document Windows

Switch
Windows ▾

1. Choose View, then CLICK   .
2. Select the document window to open.

You also can use the Windows taskbar to switch between document windows. CLICK the icon for the Office application on the taskbar, then select the document window to open.

Arranging Document Windows

The windows for an Office application can be opened side by side or cascaded.

- CLICK View, then select Arrange All to arrange windows side by side.
- CLICK View, then select Cascade to cascade windows.

Hiding, Opening and Closing Document Windows

Minimize document window so it's hidden from view (but not closed).

Maximize document window to full screen mode.

Exit full screen mode.

Close a document window. If there are unsaved changes, click Yes to save the changes.

Working with Documents

Use the File menu to manage your documents, including opening, saving, printing, sending via email and closing.

- Open the File menu by choosing File on the ribbon.

- Close the File menu by selecting 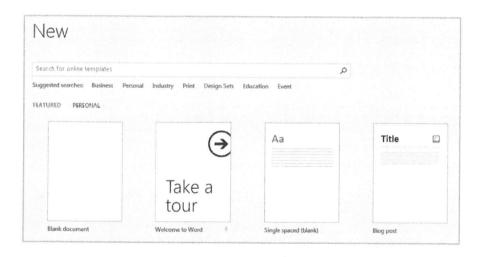, then clicking in the document or selecting a ribbon tab.

Creating a New Document

To create a blank document press CTRL + N. Or:
1. Choose File, New.
2. Select the Blank template.

Creating a New Document from a Template

1. Choose File, New.
2. Select the template to use.

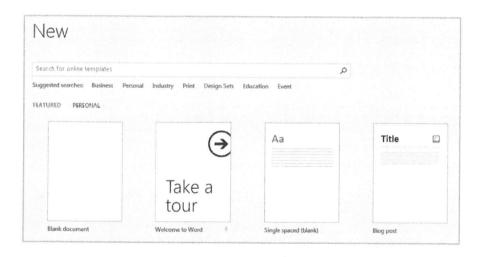

You also can find templates online by searching for the type of document you want to create. To find a template online:

1. Choose File, New.

2. Type descriptive text in the Search box, then press Enter. Use suggested searches to quickly find a particular type of document, such as a business or personal document.

Opening an Existing Document

1. Choose File, Open.

2. Select a recently opened document, or:

- Select This PC to open My Documents.
- Select OneDrive or other web locations for files stored online.
- Select Browse to search for the file to open.

3. Select a file, then CLICK Open.

Saving a Document

To overwrite a file that has already been saved:

- CLICK 🖫 on the Quick Access toolbar.
- Choose File, then Save or press CTRL + S.

If you're saving a file for the first time, see the next section.

Saving with a New Name or Location

1. Choose File, then Save As.

2. The last used location is selected by default:

- Select This PC to save to a Recent folder, My Documents or Desktop.
- Select OneDrive or other web locations to save online.
- Select Browse to search for the save location.

3. Type a file name, then CLICK Save.

Saving a PDF

The Portable Document Format (PDF) is the format used with Adobe Acrobat and Adobe Reader. After you save a document in an Office format, you can save the document as a PDF.

To create a PDF copy of a document:

1. Choose File, Export, then select

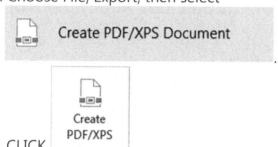

2. CLICK .
3. Type a filename, then choose a save location.
4. CLICK Publish.

Printing or Previewing a Document

1. Choose File, Print or press CTRL + P.

2. CLICK ◄ or ► to view other pages, or press Page Up or Page Down.
3. Show multiple pages by dragging the Zoom In/Out slider to the left or right until the desired number of pages is displayed.

NOTE: CLICK to return to standard page zoom.

4. As necessary, specify the number of copies to print, the printer to use, the pages to print and other print options.

5. CLICK . Or exit preview mode without printing by

CLICKING .

Sending a Document as an Email Attachment or PDF

1. Choose File, then Share.

2. CLICK Email.

3. CLICK Send as Attachment to send as an attached document. Or,

CLICK Send as PDF to send as a PDF version of the document.

4. Complete and send the email.

Working with the Status Bar

The status bar is displayed along the bottom of the window. By default, information about the document is displayed on the left and view/layout and zoom options are displayed on the right.

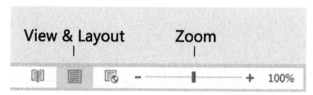

Customizing the Status Bar

RIGHT-CLICK the status bar and select display options to turn them on or off. A checkmark indicates an option is selected.

Zooming In or Out

- DRAG the Zoom slider left to reduce the zoom level (shrink).
- DRAG the Zoom slider right to increase the zoom level (enlarge).
- STRETCH or PINCH.

To use the Zoom dialog box instead:

1. Select View, then CLICK Zoom.
2. Choose a Zoom option.

Changing the View Mode

The view modes determine how you view the document and are optimized for different purposes. With Word, the View layouts are optimized for reading, printing or web viewing modes. With Excel, there are Normal, Page Layout and Page

Break views. With PowerPoint, there are Normal, Slide Sort and Reading views.

To change the view mode:

- CLICK a view button on the Status bar.
- Select View, then choose a view in the Views group.

Managing Text, Pictures and Other Items

You can insert text, pictures and other items into documents. Any inserted item has a related shortcut menu that can be used to modify or format the item.

Shortcut menus display options specific to an item, such as a misspelled word, chart or picture. To use a shortcut menu, RIGHT-CLICK on an item, then select the option from the list, or PRESS AND HOLD, then release when a box appears.

Selecting Text

- DRAG across the text to select. In Excel, first DOUBLE-CLICK to edit the cell contents.
- Hold SHIFT and use the arrow keys. To select words, hold CTRL + SHIFT and use the arrow keys.
- TAP and DRAG to change the start and end points of the selection.
- To select multiple text areas, make a selection, then hold CTRL while making additional selections.

Inserting or Deleting Text

With Excel, you must first DOUBLE-CLICK to edit the cell contents. This isn't necessary with Word or PowerPoint.

To insert text, CLICK where the text is to be inserted, then type.

To delete text, CLICK where the text is to be deleted. If the insertion point is before the text to delete, press the Delete key. If the insertion point is after the text to delete, press the Backspace key.

To delete a large section or paragraph of text, select the text area to delete, then press the Delete or Backspace key.

To replace text, select the text to replace, then type the new text.

Selecting Shapes, Pictures or Excel Cells

- CLICK on a shape, picture or Excel cell.
- To select multiple shapes, DRAG around the shapes.
- To select multiple cells in Excel, DRAG across the cells.
- To select multiple non-adjacent shapes, pictures or cells, hold CTRL while making selections.

While the shape, picture or cell is selected, you can work with it and may find a related management tab is available. RIGHT-CLICK to display management options.

Moving or Copying

1. Select the text, shape, picture, Excel cell or other item to move or copy.
2. To move the item, choose Home, then CLICK Cut or press CTRL + X. To copy the item, choose Home, then CLICK Copy or press CTRL + C.
3. CLICK to place the cursor where you want to move or copy.
4. Choose Home, then CLICK Paste or press CTRL + V.

Some items may have formatting that you want to keep, merge or discard. If so:

1. Select Home, then CLICK .
2. Choose a paste option, such as Keep Source Formatting or Keep Text Only.

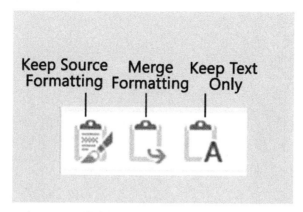

The paste options available depend on the type of item and the Office application you are using.

Dragging and Dropping

1. Select the text, shape, picture, excel cell or other item to move or copy.
2. Move by dragging to the new location. Copy by pressing CTRL while dragging.

Moving Pictures, Shapes, Etc.

To move a picture or other object, DRAG it to a new location. Or press CTRL + X to cut the item from its current location and then press CTRL + V to paste to a new location.

Deleting Shapes, Pictures or Excel Cells

1. CLICK on a shape, picture or Excel cell.
2. Press the Delete or Backspace key.

Formatting Text

Use formatting to modify the way text looks in your document. Most formatting options are on the Home tab. Remember, selecting cells or shapes then formatting will change all the text within the selected item.

Changing Text Font and Size

1. Select the text or item to change.
2. Choose Home, then select the Font to use.
3. Select a font size or type the size in the combo box provided.

Using Bold, Italic, Underline, Etc.

Text can be styled using bold, italic, underline and strikethrough options. Combine styles as appropriate and necessary.

1. Select the text or item to change.
2. Choose Home, then use the Bold, Italic, Underline and Strikethrough buttons to style the text.

The default underline style is a single line. Click the Underline Options button to select a different underline style, such as dotted underline or dashed underline.

To remove styling:

1. Select the text or item to change.
2. Choose the same styling buttons to remove the previously applied styles.

A common style you may use together is bold italic. To apply this style, you would CLICK the Bold button and then CLICK the Italic button. To subsequently remove this styling, you would select the text, then CLICK the Bold button followed by the Italic button.

Adding Text Colors

1. Select the text or item to modify.
2. Choose Home, then use the Text Color Options button to select the color.

- Clicking the Text Color button without using the Options button applies the default or last used color.

Using the Mini Style Toolbar

Use the mini style toolbar to quickly format. This toolbar is displayed beside text, cells or shapes whenever you:

- Select text with a mouse.
- RIGHT-CLICK text, cells or shapes.
- TAP selected items.

Adding Pictures, Shapes and SmartArt

The Insert tab is where you'll find options for inserting shapes, pictures and SmartArt.

Pictures Online Shapes SmartArt
         Pictures

Inserting Pictures

Office 2016 allows you to add pictures in any compatible file format, including GIF, JPG, BMP, PNG and more.

To add a picture from your computer:

Pictures

1. Select Insert, CLICK   .
2. Select a picture from your computer, then choose Insert.

To add a picture from an online resource:

Online

1. Select Insert, CLICK Pictures .
2. Search Bing or browse your OneDrive account. Or, CLICK a connected Facebook or Flickr account to browse your other online pictures.
3. Select a picture, then choose Insert.

To format a picture:

1. CLICK the picture to select it.
2. Use Picture Tools, Format to format the picture.

Drawing Shapes

Shapes provide an easy way to add geometric shapes, such as circles, stars, arrows and lines, to your documents.

To draw a shape:

Shapes

1. Select Insert, CLICK ▾ .
2. Select a shape to use.
3. CLICK and DRAG where you want to draw the shape.

To format a shape:

1. CLICK the shape to select it.
2. Use Drawing Tools, Format to format the shape.

Using SmartArt

SmartArt helps you add diagrams, organizational charts and other information graphics to your documents.

To add SmartArt:

SmartArt

1. Select Insert,   .
2. Use the Choose A SmartArt Graphic dialog box to select the art to use. CLICK a SmartArt to get a description. CLICK a SmartArt, then CLICK OK to add the art.
3. CLICK the placeholder text, then type the desired text.
4. If available, click the picture placeholder, then select the picture to add.

To format art:

1. CLICK the SmartArt to select it.
2. Use SmartArt Tools, Design to modify the art design.
3. Use SmartArt Tools, Format to modify the art format.

Making Changes and Corrections

With Office 2016, common mistakes are fixed automatically while you type, e.g. frmo is changed to from. Some text you type changes to symbols, e.g. (c) changes to ©. AutoCorrect is the feature that performs these changes.

Viewing AutoCorrect Settings

1. Choose File, Options, then select Proofing.
2. CLICK AutoCorrect Options.

- The AutoCorrect checkboxes control basic behavior. Each option with a checkmark is enabled.
- The Replace Text As You Type entries list text that is replaced and shows you the replacement value, e.g. (tm) is replaced with ™.

Modifying AutoCorrect Settings

1. Choose File, Options, then select Proofing.
2. CLICK AutoCorrect Options.
3. As appropriate, do the following:

- Clear checkboxes for AutoCorrect options you don't want to use. Select checkboxes for AutoCorrect options you want to use.
- To modify replacement behavior, locate and select an entry to modify, then enter or modify the text in the Replace and With boxes.

Checking Spelling

Word, Excel, and PowerPoint check spelling as you type. A red wavy line shows a spelling error.

To spellcheck an entire document, choose Review and then select Spelling (or Spelling & Grammar with Word).

Correct a mistake, or RIGHT-CLICK the word with the wavy line then:

- If incorrect, choose from the available suggestions.
- If correct for spelling, choose Ignore All or add the word to the Office dictionary by selecting Add To Dictionary.

Checking Grammar

Only Word checks grammar as you type. A blue wavy line shows a grammar error. To grammar check an entire document, choose Review and then select Spelling & Grammar.

Correct a mistake, or RIGHT-CLICK the word with the wavy line then:

- If incorrect, choose from the available suggestions.

- Choose Ignore Once to skip the error.

Using the Dictionary and Thesaurus

Word, Excel, and PowerPoint have a built-in dictionary and thesaurus.

1. Select a word, then choose Review.
2. For definitions, CLICK Smart Lookup, then under Insights, CLICK Define.
3. For synonyms, CLICK Thesaurus.

Undoing or Redoing Actions

Sometimes AutoCorrect will make changes you don't want. If you CLICK or press CTRL + Z immediately after the text is corrected, the change is removed.

Undo is also handy to remove formatting or other changes that you don't want. To undo a change, simply CLICK . To undo other changes, CLICK and choose the changes to undo.

To redo an action, CLICK . This reverses the Undo command. If you used Undo several times, is displayed, allowing you to choose specific changes to redo.

In Excel, you can use and to redo or undo several steps at once.

Repeating Actions

In Word and PowerPoint, changes to when there are no changes to redo. Use to repeat the last action. Alternatively, you can press CTRL + Y to repeat an action.

Managing File Formats

Office 2007 to Office 2016 use the same file format. Here, Office saves files with the file extension docx, pptx or xlsx, e.g. MyReport.docx.

The x in the filename tells you the files are stored as a special type of Zip archive that contains the elements of your document stored in separate files. In the archive, the document itself is formatted using XHTML, an extensible markup language that is based on an open standard.

Opening Files Created in Earlier Versions of Office

Office 2003 and earlier save files with the extension doc, ptt or xls. These files are stored using a proprietary formatting that is exclusive to Microsoft.

In Office 2016, you can open documents using the current or older format. Office 2016 uses a compatibility mode when opening files created with an earlier file format. Features are disabled or modified as necessary to ensure compatibility. Older Office versions also use a compatibility mode when opening newer file formats.

Saving Files Created in Earlier Versions of Office

Documents are saved by default in the format they were created in. You can easily save a document created in the old format with the new format and vice versa, e.g. a doc file can be saved as a docx file or a docx file can be saved as a doc file.

To save a file using a format other than its original format:

1. Choose File, then Save As.
2. Select a save location.
3. Type a file name.

4. Select Save As Type, then choose the type.

Checking Compatibility with Earlier Versions

Although Office 2007 to Office 2016 use the same file format, various features and options are different in each of these versions. These differences mean that sometimes your document won't work as expected in a different Office version.

To determine how your Office 2016 document will work when opened with an earlier version of Office:

1. Choose File, then Info.
2. Select Check For Issues, then select Check Compatibility.
3. To change the version to check, choose Select Versions To Show, then clear or select the checkboxes for the versions.
4. Note any problems, then CLICK OK.

Commonly Used Office Shortcuts

Bold (On/Off)	CTRL +B
Close Active Widow	CTRL + W
Close Dialog	ESC
Copy selected items	CTRL + C
Cut selected items	CTRL + X
Cycle through open windows	CTRL + TAB
Display Help	F1
Display Ribbon (Show/Hide)	ALT or F10
Find And Replace	CTRL + H
Find	CTRL + F
Insert Hyperlink	CTRL + K
Italic (On/Off)	CTRL +I
New document	CTRL + N
Open a document	CTRL + O
Paste Special	CTRL + ALT + V
Paste the clipboard contents	CTRL + V
Print a document	CTRL + P
Redo or repeat the last action	CTRL +Y

Repeat Find (after closing Find)	SHIFT + F4
Ribbon (Show/Hide)	CTRL + F1
Save As	F12
Save current document	CTRL + S
Select a paragraph	Triple Click
Select a Word	Double Click
Select All	CTRL + A
Selection Pane (Show/Hide)	ALT + F10
Shortcut Menu	SHIFT + F10
Spell Check	F7
Thesaurus	SHIFT + F7
Underline (On/Off)	CTRL +U
Undo the last action	CTRL +Z

Word 2016 Shortcuts

Text Selection Shortcuts

Select a word	DOUBLE-CLICK the word
Select a sentence	CLICK the sentence
Select a paragraph	DOUBLE-CLICK selection area beside the paragraph or TRIPLE-CLICK in paragraph
Select all text	CTRL + A
Make multiple selections	Press CTRL while making additional selections

Special Character Shortcuts

Column break	CTRL + SHIFT + Enter
Ellipsis	ALT + CTRL + period
Line break	SHIFT + Enter
Non-breaking space	CTRL + SHIFT + space
Page break	CTRL + Enter
Copyright symbol	ALT + CTRL + C
Registered trademark symbol	ALT + CTRL + R
Trademark symbol	ALT + CTRL + T

Navigation Shortcuts

Hold SHIFT with any of the navigation shortcuts to select from the current position to that position.

Beginning of document	CTRL + Home
Beginning of line	Home
End of document	CTRL + End
End of line	End
Go to page number	F5
Top of the next page	CTRL + Page Down
Top of the previous page	CTRL + Page Up

View Shortcuts

Outline view	ALT + CTRL + O
Draft view	ALT + CTRL + N
Print preview	ALT + CTRL + I
Print layout	ALT + CTRL + P

Formatting Shortcuts

All capitals (on/off)	CTRL + SHIFT + A
Apply H1 style	ALT + CTRL + 1
Apply H2 style	ALT + CTRL + 2
Apply H3 style	ALT + CTRL + 3
Apply Normal style	CTRL + SHIFT + N
Bold (on/off)	CTRL + B
Change case of letters	SHIFT + F3
Center (on/off)	CTRL + E
Decrease font size by 1 point	CTRL + [
Decrease font size	CTRL + SHIFT + <
Decrease left indent	CTRL + SHIFT + M
Display Font dialog box	CTRL + D
Double underline (on/off)	CTRL + SHIFT + D
Increase font size by 1 point	CTRL +]
Increase font size	CTRL + SHIFT + >
Increase left indent	CTRL + M
Italic (on/off)	CTRL + I

Justify (on/off)	CTRL + J
Left-align (on/off)	CTRL + L
Reveal formatting on paragraphs	SHIFT + F1
Right-align (on/off)	CTRL + R
Small capitals (on/off)	CTRL + SHIFT + K
Underline (on/off)	CTRL + U

PowerPoint 2016 Shortcuts

General Shortcuts

Change case of letters	SHIFT + F3
Collapse paragraph (outline)	ALT + SHIFT + -
Create a new slide	CTRL + M
Decrease font size	CTRL + SHIFT + <
Demote paragraph/bullet	ALT + SHIFT + ←
Display Font dialog box	CTRL + T
Duplicate selected object	CTRL + D
Expand paragraph (outline)	ALT + SHIFT + +
Grid (on/off)	SHIFT + F9
Guides (on/off)	F9
Increase font size	CTRL + SHIFT + >
Line break	SHIFT + Enter
Move to next textbox on slide	CTRL + Enter
Play a slide show	F5
Promote paragraph/bullet	ALT + SHIFT + →

Media Shortcuts

Decrease volume	ALT + Down Arrow key
Increase volume	ALT + Up Arrow key
Jump backward	ALT + SHIFT + ←
Jump forward	ALT + SHIFT + →
Mute (on/off)	ALT + U
Next bookmark	ALT + End
Pause/Play	ALT + P
Previous bookmark	ALT + Home
Stop playing	ALT + Q

Slideshow Shortcuts

Automatic show (on/off)	S or +
Black screen (on/off)	B or period
Change pointer to arrow	CTRL + A
Change pointer to pen	CTRL + P
End show	ESC
Erase screen annotations	E
First slide	Home

Go to a slide number	Press number then Enter
Go to next hyperlink	Tab
Go to previous hyperlink	SHIFT + Tab
Go to the next hidden slide (when pressed on preceding slide)	H
Hide mouse pointer	CTRL + H
Last slide	End
Next slide	Click, spacebar, N, Page Down or Enter
Previous slide	Backspace, P or Page Up
Select hyperlink	Enter
Show all slides	CTRL + S
Show shortcuts	F1
Show taskbar	CTRL + T
White screen (on/off)	W or comma

Excel 2016 Shortcuts

General Shortcuts

Insert worksheet	SHIFT + F11
Function dialog box	SHIFT + F3
Create a table	CTRL + T
Create a new line in cell	ALT + ENTER
Enter the date	CTRL + ;
Enter the time	CTRL + SHIFT + :
Name Manager	CTRL + F3
Create names from row/column labels	CTRL + SHIFT + F3
Edit the active cell	F2
Add/Edit cell comment	SHIFT + F2
Insert chart sheet based on selection	F11
Insert chart	ALT + F1
Delete selected cells	CTRL + -
Insert blank cells	CTRL + SHIFT + +

Special Character Shortcuts

Press ALT and use numeric keypad. These also work for Word and PowerPoint.

¢	ALT + 0162
£	ALT + 0163
¥	ALT + 0165
€	ALT + 0128

Selection Shortcuts

All comments	CTRL + SHIFT + O
All objects (with an object selected)	CTRL + SHIFT + spacebar
Area around active cell	CTRL + SHIFT + * or CTRL + SHIFT + spacebar
Array containing active cell	CTRL + /
Cells containing formulas that directly or indirectly reference the active cell	CTRL + SHIFT + }
Cells containing formulas that directly reference active cell	CTRL +]

Cells that don't match value in active cell (with column selected)	CTRL + SHIFT + |
Cells that don't match value in active cell (with row selected)	CTRL + \
Cells directly or indirectly referenced by formulas in the selection	CTRL + {
Cells directly referenced by formulas in the selection	CTRL + [
Column	CTRL + spacebar. Or CLICK the column heading
Named range	CLICK the name from the Name Box list
Range	Select a range, press CTRL and select additional ranges
Row	SHIFT + spacebar. Or CLICK the row heading
Visible cells in current selection (not hidden cells)	ALT + ;
Worksheet	CTRL + A

Navigation Shortcuts

Hold SHIFT with any of the navigation shortcuts to select from the current position to that position.

Beginning of current row	Home
Cell A1	CTRL + Home
Go to Cell	F5
Last filled cell (or next filled cell if in blank cell) in any direction	CTRL + arrow key
Last used column/row	CTRL + End
Next unlocked cell (in protected worksheet)	Tab
Next worksheet	CTRL + Page Down
Previous worksheet	CTRL + Page Up
Screen down	Page Down
Screen left	ALT + Page Up
Screen right	ALT + Page Down
Screen up	Page Up

Fill, Formatting & Formula Shortcuts

Format Cells dialog box	CTRL + 1
Formula palette (after entering function name in formula)	CTRL + A
Apply the Currency format	CTRL + SHIFT + $
Apply the Date format	CTRL + SHIFT + #
Apply the general number format	CTRL + SHIFT + -
Apply the Number format	CTRL + SHIFT + !
Apply the Percentage format	CTRL + SHIFT + %
Apply the Time format	CTRL + SHIFT + @
Copy formula from cell above	CTRL + SHIFT + '
Copy value from cell above	CTRL + SHIFT + "
Fill down	CTRL + D
Fill right	CTRL + R
Fill selection with current entry	CTRL + Enter
Hide columns	CTRL + 0 (zero)
Hide rows	CTRL + 9

Insert the AutoSum formula	Alt + =
Outline border	CTRL + SHIFT + &
Paste defined name into formula	F3
Remove outline border	CTRL + SHIFT + _ (underscore)
Unhide columns (with cells that include the hidden items selected)	CTRL + SHIFT +)
Unhide rows (with cells that include the hidden items selected)	CTRL + SHIFT + (

Thank you...

Thank you for purchasing this book. If you enjoyed this book and learned something from it, I hope you'll take a moment to write a review. Your reviews will help to ensure I can keep writing. If you have comments for me, a wish list for additions or feedback about a topic you'd like me to write about next, contact me by sending an email to:

OrdinaryHuman.Books@gmail.com

With your support, this book will grow and grow, so be sure to look for updates periodically! To get updated content, simply delete the book off your reader and then download again at Amazon's website.

More Books...

Ordinary Human is hard at work on other books for Microsoft products. If you'd like to see a book for a particular product, let us know!

Notes...

Notes...

Notes...

CPSIA information can be obtained
at www.ICGtesting.com
Printed in the USA
LVOW04s1612091215
466131LV00023B/1507/P

9 781517 558796